# WHAT IS GOD LIKE?

## A BOOK ABOUT GOD

Written by

Cynthia Geisen

Illustrated by

Anne FitzGerald

**ABBEY PRESS** Publications

1 Hill Drive

St. Meinrad, IN 47577

Text © 2012 Cynthia Geisen
Illustrations © 2012 St. Meinrad Archabbey
Published by Abbey Press Publications
1 Hill Drive
St. Meinrad, Indiana 47577

Library of Congress Catalog Number
2012949201

ISBN 978-0-87029-516-4

Printed in the United States of America.

# A Message from the Author
# to Parents and Caring Adults

God is a mystery. All our attempts to define or explain God inevitably fall short. The best we can do is to describe our experiences of God. Throughout time, faith-filled people have been using the language of metaphor to talk about their encounters with God. Thus, the pages of Scripture are bursting with a rich cascade of God images. In Hosea, God is portrayed as an adult teaching a toddler to walk. The psalms contain an array of God images, including a rock, a refuge, and a savior. Jesus told stories in which he described God as a mother hen, the sower of seeds, and a woman who lost (then found) a coin.

One of my favorite God images comes from 13th-century theologian Meister Eckhart. He wrote, "God is like a person who clears his throat while hiding and so gives himself away." The image of a God who plays hide-and-seek with us, shaped my approach to this book.

First, like Eckhart, I trust that God is aching to be found. Metaphors for God are like scattered bread crumbs; they clue us in to God's varied disguises. Images of God help us keep our eyes peeled for God-sightings in our daily lives. My goal in writing this book was to provide several metaphors that speak directly to children's experiences. Therefore, you will find in these pages, images of God as a crossing guard and as someone who shines a flashlight into dark and scary places.

Also, like Eckhart, I am enchanted by the notion of God's playfulness. So, in a spirit of play, the book ends by inviting you and your young reading companion to start your own list of God images. Talk together about how God is both *like* and *unlike* the images you concoct. Be creative. Fight back your urge to censor an image that startles you. Instead, use it as a springboard for conversation. My hope is that this exercise in crafting God images will launch your young reading companion on a lifelong quest for God—who so eagerly is waiting to be found.

—*Cindy Geisen*

# God is like ____

What have you heard about God?

Maybe you learned that **God is like** a loving father and we are God's children.

You might have heard that **God is like** a shepherd and we are God's sheep.

Let's find more ways to talk about God.

# God helps us when we are afraid.

Have you ever been scared in the dark?

Have you worried that monsters were hiding in your room?

**God is like** someone who shines a flashlight into dark and scary places, then sits beside you until you fall asleep.

# God wants us to be safe.

Are you careful when you ride your bike?

Do you look both ways before you cross a street or parking lot?

**God is like** a crossing guard who stops cars so you can cross the street safely.

# God forgives us.

Have you ever done something wrong?

Maybe you hurt your friend's feelings.

You might have pinched your sister.

Maybe you told a lie.

God is like someone who writes down everything we do wrong— then erases it.

# God loves to make things.

Look up at the stars. God made them.

Look down at the ground. God made it.

Look all around you. God made everything you see.

Look in the mirror. God made you.

**God is like** an inventor who keeps making beautiful things.

# God wants us to be our best.

God made each of us very good at something.

Maybe you play baseball or sing well.

You may be good at reading or adding.

**God is like** a teacher who helps us find what we do well—and grow even better at it.

# God loves us.

Have you ever seen a mother duck with her babies?

She opens her wings so her ducklings can cuddle next to her.

Her wings keep her babies warm and safe.

**God is like** a mother duck who keeps us close and safe.

# You can lean on God.

Have you rested against the trunk of a tree?

Maybe you climbed a tree and sat in its sturdy branches.

Have you played in a treehouse?

**God is like** a strong oak tree that holds us securely in its limbs.

# The world is God's art project.

Watch the sunset. How many colors do you see?

Touch the soft petals of a flower.

Listen to frogs croak and birds sing.

**God is like** an artist who made the whole world for us to enjoy and care for.

# God's love never ends.

What happens when you forget to turn off a water faucet?

The water runs and runs.

It never stops.

Water gushes over the sink and onto the floor.

**God is like** someone whose love for us never stops flowing.

# God makes room for everyone.

Have you ever been invited to a party?

Maybe an invitation came in the mail.

Or a friend said, "Please come."

It hurts when other kids are invited, but you are not.

God is like someone who hosts a party and invites EVERYONE.

# God wants us to share.

God feels sad when people are without food or clothes.

God is happy when we share food with hungry people and give away our hand-me-down clothes or toys.

**God is like** a mother who smiles when you share with your sister.

# God likes adventures.

Are you curious?

Do you enjoy visiting new places and seeing strange sights?

Do you say, "ME!" when a teacher asks, "Who wants to go first?"

**God is like** a guide who keeps us safe while we explore new paths.

# It's Your Turn!

We have found many ways to talk about God. BUT, there are still more to find!

Now it's your turn. You might:
- Start your own list of **"What God is like."**
- Draw a picture of God.
- Make up a song about God.

Remember, God loves you, no matter what!

**Cynthia Geisen** has been working in ministry for 20 years. She has served as a chaplain, as an advocate for survivors of domestic and sexual violence, and as a pastor for congregations that are in transition. She has written several publications for Abbey Press Publications.

**Anne FitzGerald** is an internationally known artist and has written and illustrated over 200 children's books. She is creator of "Dear God Kids" and many other children's books and products. Anne works from her studio/gallery in Limerick, Ireland, and teaches art in Liberty Christian School there.

For other books in this series go to:
www.abbeypresspublications.com
and click on "JUST FOR ME BOOKS" in the side bar.